AVE OGDEN!
NASH IN LATIN

AVE OGDEN! NASH IN LATIN

POEMS BY OGDEN NASH

Translated by
James C. Gleeson and Brian N. Meyer

With drawings by Ken Maryanski

LITTLE, BROWN AND COMPANY — BOSTON – TORONTO

811
N

First Edition

T 11/73

Many of these poems first appeared in magazines and are reprinted through the courtesy of the following: *Cosmopolitan, Harper's Magazine, Holiday, House & Garden, The New Yorker, Saturday Evening Post* and *Woman's Day.*

"Snap, Crackle, Pop" was originally published by *Redbook* Magazine. Copyright 1933 by The McCall Publishing Company.

Library of Congress Cataloging in Publication Data

Nash, Ogden, 1902-1971.
  Ave Ogden! Nash in Latin.

  Poems.
  English and Latin.   I.   Title.
PS3527.A637A95 1973   811'.5'2   73-13586
ISBN 0-316-31590-7

Published simultaneously in Canada by Little, Brown & Company (Canada) Limited

Printed in the United States of America

ACKNOWLEDGMENTS

For interest and encouragement, thanks are certainly due Reverend Joseph P. Dunne, John E. Emmett, Frank Geppert, Dr. Konrad Gries, Monsignor Charles E. Spence (Oxon.), and Dr. Albert E. Warsley.

CONTENTS

CONTENTAE

AVE OGDEN!
NASH IN LATIN

CANIS

Non trudo nec distendo verum
Cum dico canem amoris plenum.
Probavi vero probatione
Udum amantissimum esse.

THE DOG

The truth I do not stretch or shove
When I state the dog is full of love.
I've also proved by actual test,
A wet dog is the lovingest.

THE ASP

Whenever I behold an asp
I can't suppress a startled gasp.
I do not charge the asp with matricide,
But what about his Cleopatricide?

THE PARENT

Children aren't happy with nothing to ignore,
And that's what parents were created for.

ASPIS

Quotiens obtueor, non possum
Vincere territum anhelitum.
Non accuso aspidem matricidio,
At quid de eius Cleopatricidio?

PARENS

Liberi quibus nil neglegendum non beati,
Hanc ob rem parentes sunt creati.

CAMELUS

Camelus habet unum gibbum;
Dromedarius, duos;
Vice versa aliter.
Incertus sum. Estisne vos?

THE CAMEL

The camel has a single hump;
The dromedary, two;
Or else the other way around.
I'm never sure. Are you?

LATHER AS YOU GO

Beneath this slab
John Brown is stowed.
He watched the ads,
And not the road.

THE RABBITS

Here's a verse about rabbits
That doesn't mention their habits.

SPUMA DUM IS

M. dejectus est
Hanc sub tabulam.
Spectabat libellos
Et non viam.

LEPORES

Hic est versus de leporibus
Qui nil memorat de moribus.

PISTRIS

Multi Physici perscripsere
Pistrem lenem ut catulum!
Scio tamen hoc de pistre:
Morsum pejorem quam latratum.

THE SHARK

How many Scientists have written
The shark is gentle as a kitten!
Yet this I know about the shark:
His bite is worser than his bark.

THE MULES

In the world of mules
There are no rules.

THE PANTHER

The panther is like a leopard,
Except it hasn't been peppered.
Should you behold a panther crouch,
Prepare to say Ouch.
Better yet, if called by a panther,
Don't anther.

MULI

Mundus mulorum
Non est regularum.

PANTHERA

Panthera leopardo similis est,
Nisi quod non pipere nota est.
Si distraheris pantherae flexu,
Para dicere Heu.
Praestat vocato a panthera
Non respondera.

VENATOR

Venator se submittit obscure
Sub varia dissimulatione,
Tetrinnientem stridorem incantat
Qui blanditiam illiciis praebat.
Adultus fortuna et fortitudine
Sperat anatem excellere.

THE HUNTER

The hunter crouches in his blind
'Neath camouflage of every kind,
And conjures up a quacking noise
To lend allure to his decoys.
This grown-up man, with pluck and luck,
Is hoping to outwit a duck.

THE CALF

Pray, butcher, spare yon tender calf!
Accept my plea on his behalf;
He's but a babe, too young by far
To perish in the abattoir.
Oh, cruel butcher, let him feed
And gambol on the verdant mead;
Let clover tops and grassy banks
Fill out those childish ribs and flanks.
Then may we, at some future meal,
Pitch into beef instead of veal.

VITULUS

Obsecro, lani, parce vitulo!
Accipe meam orationem pro eo;
Nimis parvus in infantia
Ut pereat in ista laniena.
O, lani saeve, sine eum ludere
Et pasci in prato viride;
Sine aggeres herbosos et trifolia
Implere pueriles costas et ilia.
Ad quasdam futuras epulas inde,
Oppugnemus bubulam loco vitulae.

OLD MEN

People expect old men to die,
They do not really mourn old men.
Old men are different. People look
At them with eyes that wonder when . . .
People watch with unshocked eyes;
But the old men know when an old man dies.

THE PORCUPINE

Any hound a porcupine nudges
Can't be blamed for harboring grudges.
I know one hound that laughed all winter
At a porcupine that sat on a splinter.

SENES

Homines exspectant morituros senes,
Non vere lugent senes illi.
Senes diversi. Homines spectant
Oculis mirantibus quando ei . . .
Impercussis oculis observant homines;
Sed senem mori sciunt senes.

HYSTRIX

Canis quem hystrix fodicat non debet
Culpari quia invidias habet.
Est unus qui totam hiemem riserit
Hystricem quae assulae insederit.

CITY GREENERY

If you should happen after dark
To find yourself in Central Park,
Ignore the paths that beckon you
And hurry, hurry to the zoo,
And creep into the tiger's lair.
Frankly, you'll be safer there.

URBANI VIRIDES

Si accidat ut te invenias
In Hortis Centralibus sub tenebras,
Neglege tramites vocantes te
In hortos zoölogicos contende,
Repe, ibi in cubilem tigris.
Vere, illic tutior eris.

PORCUS

Porcus, nisi falsus sum,
Praebet nobis pernam, lardum.
Ceteri dicant pectus amplum—
Ego dico porcum simplum.

THE PIG

The pig, if I am not mistaken,
Supplies us sausage, ham, and bacon.
Let others say his heart is big—
I call it stupid of the pig.

THE PHOENIX

Deep in the study
Of eugenics
We find that fabled
Fowl, the Phoenix.
The wisest bird
As ever was,
Rejecting other
Mas and Pas,
It lays one egg,
Not ten or twelve,
And when it's hatched it,
Out pops itself.

PHOENIX

Alti in studio
Eugeniarum
Invenimus Phoenicem
Avem fabularum.
Sapientissima
Omnium avis quae
Reicit alias
Matres Patresque,
Unum ovum parit,
Non novem nec decem,
Postquam id exclusit,
Exsilit ipsa eadem.

THE OCTOPUS

Tell me, O Octopus, I begs,
Is those things arms, or is they legs?
I marvel at thee, Octopus;
If I were thou, I'd call me Us.

THE TERMITE

Some primal termite knocked on wood
And tasted it, and found it good,
And that is why your Cousin May
Fell through the parlor floor today.

OCTIPES

Peto, Octope, mi narra,
est* illa bracchia an crura?
Admiror te, tu Octope;
Si ego tu, Nos vocarem me.

PESTIS

Prisa pestis lignum pulsavit,
Gustavit, bonum id repperit.
Quoque audimus Maiam hodie
Per solum exedri cecidisse.

* To conform with Nash's singular verb with plural noun.

WHAT'S THE USE?

Sure, deck your lower limbs in pants;
Yours are the limbs, my sweeting.
You look divine as you advance—
Have you seen yourself retreating?

THE DUCK

Behold the duck.
It does not cluck.
A cluck it lacks.
It quacks.
It is specially fond
Of a puddle or pond.
When it dines or sups,
It bottoms ups.

QUAM OB REM?

Certe, orna crura bracis;
Membra tua sunt, deliciae.
Veniens divina videris—
Vidistine abeuntem te?

ANAS

Anas ecce.
Eum non glocire.
Glogocitu eget.
Tetrinnit.
Amat praesertim
Lacunam aut stagnum.
Cum prandet aut cenat
Sursum fundum dat.

HIPPOPOTAMUS

Ecce hippopotamus, sis!
Ridemus quomodo videatur nobis,
Tempore tamen miserabili
Miror quomodo videamur ei.
Pacem, pacem, hippopotame!
Videmur grati nobis vere,
Es dulcis sine dubio
Aliorum hipporum oculo.

THE HIPPOPOTAMUS

Behold the hippopotamus!
We laugh at how he looks to us,
And yet in moments dank and grim
I wonder how we look to him.
Peace, peace, thou hippopotamus!
We really look all right to us,
As you no doubt delight the eye
Of other hippopotami.

REFLECTIONS ON ICE-BREAKING

Candy
Is dandy
But liquor
Is quicker.

THE TURTLE

The turtle lives 'twixt plated decks
Which practically conceal its sex.
I think it clever of the turtle
In such a fix to be so fertile.

MEDITATIONES DE GLACIEM RUMPENDO

Sacch'rum
Est gratum
Sed liquor
Celerior.

TESTUDO

Testudines inter bracteatos pontes habitant
Qui fere eorum sexum dissimulant.
Mihi videtur esse ingeniosum testudinem
Angustis talibus tam esse fertilem.

CANTUS VIAE APERTAE

Credo me spectaturum numquam
Tabulam ut arborem pulchram.
Nisi tabulae cadent vero,
Numquam cernam arborem omnino.

SONG OF THE OPEN ROAD

I think that I shall never see
A billboard lovely as a tree.
Indeed, unless the billboards fall
I'll never see a tree at all.

THE CENTIPEDE

I objurgate the centipede,
A bug we do not really need.
At sleepy-time he beats a path
Straight to the bedroom or the bath.
You always wallop where he's not,
Or, if he is, he makes a spot.

THE ANT

The ant has made himself illustrious
Through constant industry industrious.
So what?
Would you be calm and placid
If you were full of formic acid?

CENTIPEDA

Objurgo centipedam, quam
Non requirimus cimicem.
Hora somni facit viam
Ad cubic'lum, lavationem.
Semper locum ubi abest feris,
Quodsi ad-, is facit labīs.

FORMICA

Formica se facit illustrem
Per constantem assiduitatem.
Quid ita?
Essetisne vos sedati et placidi
Si pleni essetis formicini acidi?

LARUS

Audisne? Vagit ille larus;
Is flet quoniam non est barrus.*
Puta esse te, inepte lare,
Possis maritae explicare?

THE SEA-GULL

Hark to the whimper of the sea-gull;
He weeps because he's not an ea-gull.
Suppose you were, you silly sea-gull,
Could you explain it to your she-gull?

* Barrus: elephant, but the sense is similar.

THE PURIST

I give you now Professor Twist,
A conscientious scientist.
Trustees exclaimed, "He never bungles!"
And sent him off to distant jungles.
Camped on a tropic riverside,
One day he missed his loving bride.
She had, the guide informed him later,
Been eaten by an alligator.
Professor Twist could not but smile.
"You mean," he said, "a crocodile."

DILIGENTIOR

Trado nunc Doctorem Torquatum,
Physicum religiosum.
"Non errat," custodes clamaverunt
Ad longinquos saltus miserunt.
Ad ripam sese positus tropicam,
Olim requisiit amantem nuptam.
Ductor eam dixit deinde
Esam esse ab alligatore.
Torquatus ridere poterat solum.
"Vis dicere," inquit, "crocodilum."

COLUBER

Hoc animal implet os veneno
Et it in ejus duodeno.
Qui colubrem ludere conatur
Mox est tristior et sedatior.

THE COBRA

This creature fills its mouth with venum
And walks upon its duodenum.
He who attempts to tease the cobra
Is soon a sadder he and sobra.

THE CANARY

The song of canaries
Never varies,
And when they're moulting
They're pretty revolting.

THE FLY

God in his wisdom made the fly
And then forgot to tell us why.

FRINGILLA CANARIA

Fringillarum cantus
Numquam dilatus,
Cum pennas effundunt
Foedae nonnil sunt.

MUSCA

Deus muscam fecit prudens
Non fatus causam, obliviscens.

THE POULTRIES

Let's think of eggs.
They have no legs.
Chickens come from eggs
But they have legs.
The plot thickens;
Eggs come from chickens,
But have no legs under 'em.
What a conundrum!

PECORA VOLATILIA

Putemus ova.
Non habent crura.
Ex ovis pulli
At crura illi.
Involvitur ea;
E pullis ova,
At nulla crura infra.
Quale aenigma!

SNAP, CRACKLE, POP

Breakfast foods grow odder and odder;
It's a wise child that knows its fodder.

MAYBE YOU CAN'T TAKE IT WITH YOU, BUT LOOK WHAT HAPPENS WHEN YOU LEAVE IT BEHIND

As American towns and cities I wander through,
One landmark is constant everywhere I roam;
The house the Banker built in nineteen-two,
Dim neon tells me is now a funeral home.

STREP., CREP., ET FRAG.

Cibi fiunt praviores ad ientaculum;
Sap. est puer qui cognoscat pabulum.

FORTASSE FERRE TECUM NON POTES, SED VIDE QUID ACCIDAT CUM ID TU RELINQUAS

Cum vicos pervagor Americanas urbesque,
Est terminus quidam constans ubicumque;
Mensarius quam domum pridem conficit,
Neon nunc esse Libitinam mi dicit.

MEDICUS SENEX VALENTINUS FILIO

Superabunt qui consulunt aegri;
Morientur qui consulunt integri.
Cupio unum verbum dare
Hoc: mirare quaerereque quare.

OLD DR. VALENTINE TO HIS SON

Your hopeless patients will live,
Your healthy patients will die.
I have only this one word to give:
Wonder, and find out why.

THE KITTEN

The trouble with a kitten is
THAT
Eventually it becomes a
CAT.

THE FIREFLY

The firefly's flame
Is something for which science has no name.
I can think of nothing eerier
Than flying around with an unidentified glow on a person's posteerier.

CATULUS

Ea questio catulo
SIT
Denique iste feles
FIT.

PYROPHORUS NOCTILUCUS

Pyrophori noctiluci lumen
Per scientiam habet nullum nomen.
Possum nihil fingere mirius
Quam passim volare cum imagnito ardore in clunibus.

THE POMEGRANATE

The hardest fruit upon this planet
Is easily the ripe pomegranate.
I'm halfway through the puzzle game
Of guessing how it got its name.
The pome part turns my cowlick hoary,
But the granite is self-explanatory.

MALUM PUNICUM

Malum durissimum hac planeta tempest-
Ivum malum Punicum facile est.
In medio aenigma-ludo sum
Divinans quomodo accipiat vocabulum.
Parte Punica cirrus canescit,
Pars mala tamen se exponit.

CAUTIO CUIQUE

Considera alcedinem. Quare?
Evadens exstinctus quia quomodo volaret oblitus est et solum poterat am-
bulare.
Considera hominem, qui fortasse exstinctus evadet
Quia quomodo ambularet oblitus est et volare didicit antequam putavet.*

A CAUTION TO EVERYBODY

Consider the auk;
Becoming extinct because he forgot how to fly, and could only walk.
Consider man, who may well become extinct
Because he forgot how to walk and learned how to fly before he thinked.

* The verb form is intentionally incorrect.

SHOO, SHOO, SHOEMAKER

I often grieve for Uncle Hannibal
Who inadvertently became a cannibal.
He asked Aunt Mary to roast him the gobbler;
She understood him to say, the cobbler.

THE CHERUB

I like to watch the clouds roll by,
And think of cherubs in the sky;
But when I think of cherubim,
I don't know if they're her or him.

CEDE, CEDE, CERDO

Doleo Patruum Hannibalem frequenter
Qui anthropophagus factus imprudenter.
Petivit Amitam torrere gall'pavonem;
Credidit eum dixisse cerdonem.

CHERUB

Juvat me nubes labentes spectare
Et cherubim in caelo cogitare;
Cum cherubim cogitantur a me,
Nescio utrum sint hi aut hae.

EXPERIMENT DEGUSTATORY

A gourmet challenged me to eat
A tiny bit of rattlesnake meat,
Remarking, "Don't look horror-stricken,
You'll find it tastes a lot like chicken."
It did.
Now chicken I cannot eat
Because it tastes like rattlesnake meat.

THE SHREW

Strange as it seems, the smallest mammal
Is the shrew, and not the camel.
And that is all I ever knew,
Or wish to know, about the shrew.

EXPERIMENTUM DEGUSTATIONE

Gustator quidam sapiens
Hortatus est ut patiens
Serpentis hanc carunculam
Libarem perquam parvulam.
"Non ictus," inquit, "horrore videre,
Invenies veluti gallinam sapere."
Et sapuit.
Nunc est gallina inedulis mihi
Quod ea sapit ut caro crotali.

SOREX

Mirabiliter, minimus mammalis
Sorex est, et non camelus.
Quod est totum quod ego umquam
Scivi aut scire de sorice cupiam.

HOW TO GET ALONG WITH YOURSELF,
or
I RECOMMEND SOFTENING OF THE OUGHTERIES

When I was young I always knew
The meretricious from the true.
I was alert to call a halt
On other people's every fault.
My creed left no more chance for doubt
Than station doors marked IN and OUT.
A prophet with righteousness elated,
Dogmatic and opinionated,
Once self-convinced, I would not budge;
I was indeed a hanging judge.
I admitted, in either joy or sorrow,
No yesterday and no tomorrow.
My summary of life was reckoned
By what went on that very second.
I scoffed when kindly uncles and aunts
Said age would teach me tolerance,
For tolerance implies a doubt
That IN is IN and OUT is OUT.
But now that I am forty-nine
I'm tolerant, and like it fine.
Since the faults of others I condone,
I can be tolerant of my own.
I realize the sky won't fall

AD CONGRUENDUM TECUM,
seu
COMMENDO MOLLIENDA DEBITA

Adulescens semper scivi
Speciosum a vero esse ubi.
Excitatus dixi moram
Ad omnem aliorum culpam.
Fides non plus dubia
Quam signatae januae INTUS, EXTRA.
Vates aequitate elatus
Superbus et existimatus
Non cederem, mihi creditans;
Judex eram condemnans.
Admisi, gaudio et dolore,
Nec diem esse cras nec here.
Summatio vitae erat noto
Quod accidit et ipso puncto.
Amitas etiam Patruos qui
Me fati toleraturum risi.
Quis toleret et dubitet
Ut IN sit IN, EX sit EX et.
Quinquaginta nunc sum paene
Aequo spiritu sum bene.
Culpas aliorum condono
Culpas meas etiam ego.
Caelum non casurum gnosco

If I don't pay my bills at all.
The King of Sweden it will not irk
To hear that I neglect my work,
And tombfuls of historic dead
Care not how late I lie abed.
Oh, tolerance is the state of grace
Where everything falls into place,
So now I tolerantly think
I could tolerate a little drink.

Si non pecuniam dissolvo.
Regem Sueciae non pigebit
Ut opus neglegendum sit.
Et sepulchra mortuorum
Nil me morantur dormiturum.
O, tolerare est beatum
Ubi omne cadit statum.
Nunc me tolerante puto
Tolerantem posse laetum poclo.

YOU AND ME AND P. B. SHELLEY

What is life? Life is stepping down a step or sitting in a chair
And it isn't there.
Life is not having been told that the man has just waxed the floor,
It is pulling doors marked PUSH and pushing doors marked PULL and not
noticing notices which say PLEASE USE OTHER DOOR.
It is when you diagnose a sore throat as an unprepared geography lesson and
send your child weeping to school only to be returned an hour later covered
with spots that are indubitably genuine,
It is a concert with a trombone soloist filling in for Yehudi Menuhin.
Were it not for frustration and humiliation
I suppose the human race would get ideas above its station.
Somebody once described Shelley as a beautiful and ineffective angel beating
his luminous wings against the void in vain,
Which is certainly describing with might and main,
But probably means that we are all brothers under our pelts,
And Shelley went around pulling doors marked PUSH and pushing doors
marked PULL just like everybody else.

ME ET TE ET P. B. SHELLEY

Quis vivit? Is qui degreditur gradum, vel sedet in sella,
Et ibi non ea.
Is qui non dictus virum solum recentissime cerasse,
Is qui tradit januas signatas URGE et urget januas signatas TRAHE, et non
animadvertit titulos dicentes ALTERA JANUA UTERE.
Is qui cognoscit dolorem juguli esse geographicam lectionem imparatam et
mittit puerum lacrimantem ad ludum tantum ut revertatur hora posteriore
aspersus notis veris verissime,
Is qui audit concentum trombe labente organici pro Yehudi Menuhin trans-
ferentis se.
Nisi essent frustratio atque humiliatio
Putarem ut humanitatis imagines essent superiores quam statio.
Quidam olim descripsit Shelley pulchrum et inefficacem caelicolam plaudentem
alas fulgentes contra vacuum frustra,
Describens manibus pedibusque vera,
Quae indicent nos omnes fratres esse sub pellibus,
Et Shelley circuibat trahens januas URGE, urgens illas TRAHE aliis simil-
limus omnibus.

ALLOW ME, MADAM, BUT IT WON'T HELP

Adorable is an adjective and womankind is a noun,
And I often wonder why, although adorable womankind elects to talk stand-
ing up, it elects to put on its coat sitting down.
What is the outstanding characteristic of matinees, tea rooms, and table
d'hôtes?
Women, sitting firmly and uncomfortably on their coats;
Women at whose talents a contortionist would hesitate to scoff
Because they also sat down on their coats to take them off.
What is *savoir-faire?*
It is the ability to pick up eighty-five cents in nickels and a lipstick with the
right hand while the left hand is groping wildly over the back of a chair.
Yes, and if you desire *savoir-faire* that you could balance a cup on,
Consider the calmness of a woman trying to get her arm into the sleeve of a
coat that she has sat down too far up on.
Women are indeed the salt of the earth,
But I fail to see why they daily submit themselves voluntarily to an operation
that a man only undergoes when he is trying to put on his trousers in an
upper berth.

PERMITTE, ERA, SED NON JUVABIT

Adoranda est adjectivum, feminitas est nomen,
Et saepe miror cur, adoranda feminitas legat dicere adstans, legat induere
  vestem sedens tamen.
Quid est illud proprium spectaculi, epulae, theae conclavis?
Feminae, persedentes et incommode ad vestis;
Feminae quarum contortor dubitaret despicere talentis
Quia ut detrahant quoque sederunt ad vestis.
Scire-faciendum?
Facultas ad octoginta quinque centesimas et labri stylum colligendum dextra,
  sinistra praetendente furiose super sellae tergum.
Immo, et si desiderares scire-faciendum in quo libres poculum,
Considera quietem feminae conantis ponere bracchium in vestem, in quam
  adsedit longius sursum.
Feminae sunt sal terrarum certe,
Sed deficior intellegere cur cotidie submittant se libenter operi quod vir modo
  patiatur conans bracas induere lecto superiore.

FRUGALIS CANTATRIX

Frugalis cantatrix ornata
Cui stola quadratis notata
Et albis et caerulis
Scripsit cantionis
Ea uti cantaret contrita.

A THRIFTY SOPRANO OF HINGHAM

A thrifty soprano of Hingham
Designed her own dresses of gingham.
On the blue and white squares
She wrote opera airs
So when they wore out she could singham.

AGNUS

Agne, num scis
Saliens ubi sis?
In mentae agello.
Nunc te impello.
Agne,
Apage!

THE LAMB

Little gamboling lamb,
Do you know where you am?
In a patch of mint.
I'll give you a hint.
Scram,
Lamb!

THE ANNIVERSARY

A marriage aged one
Is hardly begun;
A fling in the sun,
But it's hardly begun;
A green horse,
A stiff course,
And leagues to be run.

A marriage aged five
Is coming alive;
Watch it wither and thrive;
Though its coming alive,
You must guess,
No or yes,
If it's going to survive.

A marriage aged ten
Is a hopeful Amen;
It's pray for it then,
And mutter Amen,
As the names
Of old flames
Sound again and again.

At twenty a marriage
Discovers its courage.
This year do not disparage,

DIES SOLLEMNIS

Conjugium annuum
Est vix inceptum;
Soli saltatum
At vix inceptum;
Viride,
Diffic'le,
Et mille currendum.

Quinque id init
Et vivere coepit;
Languescit, vigescit;
Et vivere init.
Tibi conjectum
Utrum responsum
Num superstes erit.

Conjugium decem
Est spe nuntiatum;
Id tunc orandum,
Amenque dicendum,
Appellatae
Amatoriae
Iam sonant iterum.

Ad viginti annos
Invenit animos.
Noli deterere hos annos,

It is comely in courage;
Past the teens,
And blue jeans,
It's a promising marriage.

Yet before twenty-one
It has hardly begun.
How tall in the sun,
Yet hardly begun!
But once come of age,
Pragmatically sage,
Oh, blithe to engage
Is sweet marri-age.

Tilt a twenty-first cup
To a marriage grown up,
Now sure and mature,
And securely grown up.
Raise twenty-one cheers
To the silly young years,
While I sit out the dance
With my dearest of dears.

Sunt pulchri animos.
Ultra juventas
Et bracas caeruleas
Est spe bona amos.

Ante viginti et unum
Est vix inceptum.
In sole altum,
At vix inceptum.
Sed semel pervenit
Pragmatice gnoscit.
Id quod dulce fit
O quam laetum pacit.

Proclinate poculum
Ad conjugium adultum
Nunc durum, maturum,
Secure adultum.
Levate plausos
Ad fatuos annos
Dum sedeo ego
Cum -issima dulcium.

EHEU! FUGACES,
or
WHAT A DIFFERENCE A LOT OF DAYS MAKE

When I was seventeen or so,
I scoffed at money-grubbers.
I had a cold contempt for dough,
And I wouldn't wear my rubbers.
No aspirin I took for pains,
For pests no citronella,
And in the Aprilest of rains
I carried no umbrella.

When I was young I was Sidney Carton,
Proudly clad in a Spartan tartan.
Today I'd be, if I were able,
Just healthy, wealthy, and comfortable.

When I was young I would not yield
To comforters and bed socks,
In dreams I covered center field
For the Giants or the Red Sox.
I wished to wander hence and thence,
From diamond mine to gold field,
Or piloting a Blitzen Benz,
Outdistance Barney Oldfield.

When I subscribed to *The Youth's Companion*
I longed to become a second D'Artagnan.

MY! HOW TIME FLIES,
seu
QUANTA DIFFERENTIA POST PLURES DIES

Cum circa septendecim eram,
Runcatores ridebam.
Contemnabam pecuniam,
Et calceos non gerebam.
Medicamentum non sumpsi,
Pestibus nec citronellam,
Aprili pluviis ipsi
Portavi nec umbellam.

Sidney Carton fui adulescens,
Superbe sag'lum Spartanum gerens.
Essem vero si possem hodie,
Et sanus, divesque commodie.

Adulescens me non tradidi
Lodicibus, tibialibus.
In somniis ager curandus mihi
Pro Titanis, Rubris Pedalibus.
Volui huc illucque errare,
Ex adamantis ad auri fodinam,
Aut Blitzen Benz id gubernare,
Celerior Barney Oldfield quam.

Cum cepi *Juvenis Socius*
Volui fieri D'Artagnan alius.

Today I desire a more modest label:
He's healthy, wealthy, and comfortable.

When I was pushing seventeen,
I hoped to bag a Saracen;
Today should one invade the scene,
I'd simply find it embaracen.

Ah, Postumus, no wild duck I,
But just a waddling puddle duck,
So here's a farewell to the open sky
From a middle-aged fuddy-duddle duck.

When I was young I was Roland and Oliver,
Nathan Hale and Simón Bolívar.
Today I would rather side step trouble,
And be healthy, wealthy, and comfortubble.

Modicius nomen volo hodie:
Est sanus divesque commodie.

Cum accedebam septendecim,
Ah, capiendum Saracenum;
Nunc si ille inveneret me,
Ruborem distractio afferet me.

O, Postume, nullus ferus sum,
Sed modo anatis in modo eo,
Et hic est Vale ad caelum apertum
Ab anate importuno aetatis in medio.

Fui adulescens Roland Oliverque,
Nathan Hale, Simon Bolivarque.
Problema hodie praeterirem potius,
Et sanus divesque et valde commodius.*

---

* Should be *commodus* but word was coined to agree with Nash's "comfortubble."

FABULAE OBLITAE BULFINCH
Tertium Decimum Opus Herculis

Alii putant nasum Sphingis planatum a Napoleonibus iaculatoribus
Sed non fuit, non annorum milibus.
Honor debetur homini simili Primo veste, dictu Pericli.
Hic cognitus est ut Hercules nobis et illiteratis Graecis ut Heracles,
Et Hercules egit duodecim opera fabulosissima.
Quod effecit, mi di etiam dea, exclamare incolas Thule Ultima.
Et vix putabat se opera finire narrabaturque a deis, complures patrueles
    quorum,
Aliud ut pistori iaciendum.
Omne lacerti nihil mentisque facit surdum semideum ut non immortalis factus
    sit
Nisi Sphingem ter frustratus sit.
Et Hercules dixit, Habebo rostrum anatis!
Est casus ut sim vindicator mei Oedipodis.
Ora vultumque false jucundum retinet,
Rogavit Sphingem, Quis est pugnator ponderosissimus? et ea, Ezzard
    Charles, et jam is, Non ezzet.
Et ille, Tibi dabo os ut lacessatur ad,
Cur Orpheus desiit esse phonascus et abiicit scipionem? et illa, Contendo te
    ipsum non scire, et ille, Quod plures Bacchantes quam fusti minaretur ad,
Et illa Sphinx, Non petes confundere me ter ordine, et ille, Domum plenam,
    lacunam plenam, non potes capere crateram plenam, potesne cernere mihi
    id sine nisu?
Et illa, Fumum? et Hercules dixit, Nolo, gratias, in exercitu.
Ex temporis puncto
Nasus Sphingis ex coniuncto.

FABLES BULFINCH FORGOT
The Thirteenth Labor of Hercules

Some people think the nose of the Sphinx was flattened by Napoleon's can-
noneers,

But it wasn't, not by several thousand years.

Credit should go to a person who dressed like Adam and talked like Pericles,

This person being known to us as Hercules and to the illiterate Greeks as
Heracles,

And Hercules performed twelve fabulous labors,

Which caused all the inhabitants of Ultima Thule to exclaim Begorra and
Bejabers,

And just when he thought he was through with labors he was told by the
gods, several of whom were his cousin,

That he must make it a baker's dozen.

They said that all brawn and no brain makes a dull demigod, so on immor-
tality it was no dice

Unless he stumped the Sphinx thrice,

And Hercules said, Well I'll be a duck-billed platypus,

Here is a chance to avenge my friend Oedipus,

And he assumed an expression deceptively pleasant,

And he asked the Sphinx, Who is the heavyweight champion? and she said,
Ezzard Charles, and he said, No it ezzant,

And he said, I'll give you another bone to pick at,

Why did Orpheus give up conducting and throw away his baton? and she
said, I bet you don't know, either, and he said, Because there were more
Bacchantes than he could shake a stick at.

And the Sphinx said, You can't stump me three times in a row, and he said,

A house full, a hole full, you cannot catch a bowlful, can you riddle me that
without straining?
And she said, Smoke? and Hercules said, No thank you, I'm in training.
From that point
The Sphinx's nose has been out of joint.

FABLES BULFINCH FORGOT
Medusa and the Mot Juste

Once there was a Greek divinity of the sea named Ceto and she married a man
    named Phorcus,

And the marriage must have been pretty raucous;

Their remarks about which child took after which parent must have been full
    of asperities,

Because they were the parents of the Gorgons, and the Graeae, and Scylla,
    and the dragon that guarded the apples of the Hesperides.

Bad blood somewhere.

Today the Gorgons are our topic, and as all schoolboys including you and me
    know,

They were three horrid sisters named Medusa and Euryale and Stheno,

But what most schoolboys don't know because they never get beyond their
    Silas Marners and their Hiawathas,

The Gorgons were not only monsters, they were also highly talented authors.

Medusa began it;

She wrote *Forever Granite.*

But soon Stheno and Euryale were writing, too, and they addressed her in
    daily choruses,

Saying we are three literary sisters just like the Brontës so instead of Gorgons
    why can't we be brontësauruses?

Well, Medusa may have been mythical but she wasn't mystical,

She was selfish and egotistical.

She saw wider vistas

Than simply being the sister of her sisters.

She replied, tossing away a petrified Argonaut on whom she had chipped a
    molar,

FABULAE OBLITAE BULFINCH
Medusa et Accuratio

Olim fuit maris numen Graecum nomine Ceto et nupsit homini nomine Phor-
cus,

Et connubium essendum fuit raucius;

Eorum dicta de quo adulescente simile cui parenti implenda sunt asperitatinus,

Quod fuerunt parentes Gorgonis et Graeae et Scyllae et draconis quae custo-
deret poma Hesperidum.

Malus sanguis alicubi.

Hodie Gorgones sunt argumentum nostrum, et ut omnes discipuli intellegunt
una cum me et te,

Fuerunt tres sorores horribillimae: Medusa, Stheno, Euryale.

Sed plurimi discipuli nesciunt, quod numquam peragunt suas S. Marneros et
Hiawathas,

Gorgones non solum monstras, sed etiam peritas auctoresas.

Medusa Incepit.

Rupem Perennem scripsit.

Sed mox Stheno et Euryale scribebant quoque et appellabant eam versus
cotidie,

Cantantes: Nos sumus tres eruditae sorores simillimae Brontibus itaque
praeter Gorgones cur non possumus Brontësauruses esse?

Di, fortasse fuerit fabulosa sed certe non mystica,

Sui amans et putida.

Videbat prospectum latiorem

Quam se esse sororum sororem.

Respondit, jaciens lapiditum Argonautam in quo dolavit molarem,

Vos duae esse potestis quidquid velitis, sed cum sim caseus magnus in hac
familia, malo memorare me Zolam Gorgonem.

You two can be what you like, but since I am the big *fromage* in this family, I prefer to think of myself as the Gorgon Zola.

INDEX OF FIRST LINES